First Science

Amazing Magnets

Editorial planning: Serpentine Editorial
Scientific consultant: Dr. J.J.M. Rowe

Designed by The R & B Partnership
Illustrator: David Anstey
Photographer: Peter Millard

Additional photographs:
ZEFA 25, 30 (bottom);
Bruce Iverson/Science Photo Library 19;
Sinclair Stammers/Science Photo Library 30 (top);
Pacific Press Service/Science Photo Library 31 (top).

Library of Congress Cataloging-in-Publication Data

Rowe, Julian.
    Amazing magnets / by Julian Rowe and Molly Perham.
      p.   cm. — (First science)
    Includes index.
    ISBN 0-516-08137-3
      1. Magnets—Experiments—Juvenile literature. 2. Magnetism—Experiments—
Juvenile literature. [1. Magnets—Experiments. 2. Magnetism—Experiments.
3. Experiments.] I. Perham, Molly. II. Title. III. Series: First science (Chicago, Ill.)
    QC757.5.R69 1994
    538.4'078—dc20   94-16942
                                                                                 CIP
                                                                                  AC

First Science

Amazing Magnets

Julian Rowe
and Molly Perham

CHILDRENS PRESS®

CHICAGO

Contents

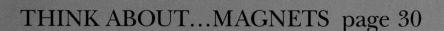
 SAFETY WARNING

Activities marked with this symbol require the presence
and help of an adult.

Is it magnetic?

Collect some small objects of different materials, like a fork, paper clips, nails, and pins. Hold a magnet over each object.

Some of the objects stick to the magnet.

A magnet pulls toward it, or attracts, things made of iron. Iron is a magnetic material. Some other metals are also magnetic.

Other things do not stick to the magnet.

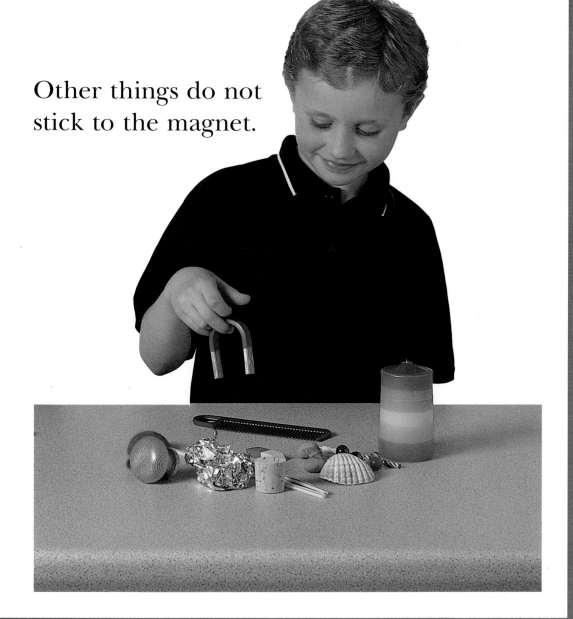

Pulling power

Hold a magnet close to a refrigerator door.
Can you feel it being pulled toward the door?
Let go and see the magnet stick to the door.

The refrigerator door is made
of steel, which contains iron.

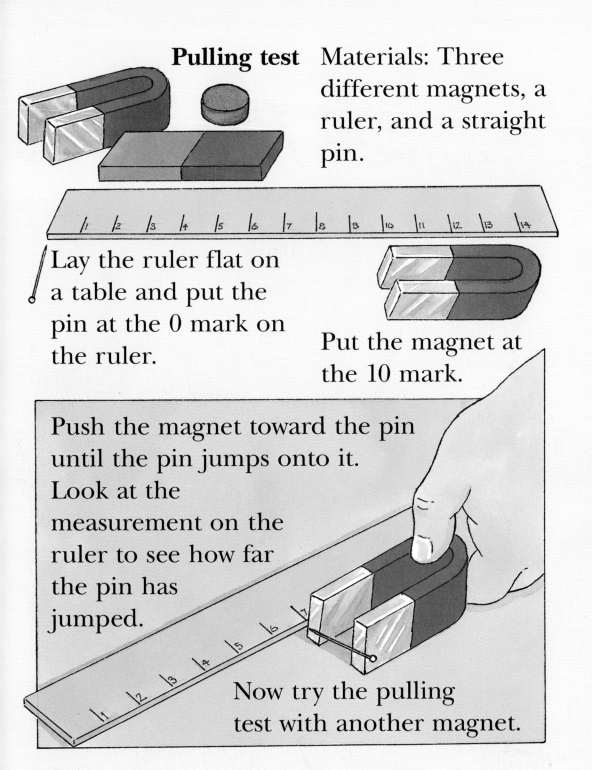

Pulling test Materials: Three different magnets, a ruler, and a straight pin.

Lay the ruler flat on a table and put the pin at the 0 mark on the ruler.

Put the magnet at the 10 mark.

Push the magnet toward the pin until the pin jumps onto it. Look at the measurement on the ruler to see how far the pin has jumped.

Now try the pulling test with another magnet.

Which magnet attracts the pin from farther away?

More and more magnets

Some magnets are stronger than others. This magnet easily picks up steel paper clips from the table. Some of the paper clips are sticking to each other.

This strong magnet can pick up several spoons.

See how each spoon has become magnetized. Each spoon acts like a magnet and attracts other spoons.

Magnetic games

Have you ever played with a magnetic game? These boys are playing with magnetic chips.

The chips stick to the board. Even if the boys tip the board, the chips do not fall off.

Make a toy theater

Materials: A small round magnet, a ruler, masking tape, a shoe box, some corks, thumb tacks, scissors, cardboard, and crayons.

Draw some cardboard figures. Add a tab at the bottom. Color them and cut them out. Ask an adult to cut a slot in the top of each cork. Push the cardboard figures into the slots.

Push a thumb tack into the bottom of each cork. Tape the magnet to the ruler.

Slide the magnet around under the shoe box to make the figures move.

13

Magnets underwater

Magnets can attract magnetic materials through water.

Materials: A magnet, corks, thumb tacks, straight pins, masking tape, colored paper, scissors, and a plastic bowl.

Make magnetic boats

Push a thumb tack into each cork. Cut out some paper sails. Stick them on the pins with masking tape. Push the pins into the cork.

Fill the bowl with water and sail your cork boats. Hold the magnet underwater.

Can you move the boats around without touching them?

Useful magnets

A magnet also attracts through glass. One part of this magnetic window cleaner is outside the window and the other part is inside. The two parts are held together by a strong magnet.

Many of the things we use every day have magnets inside them.

A cassette player and its earphones both contain magnets.

The tape you play in your cassette player has a pattern of tiny magnets on it. When the tape is played, the cassette player changes the magnetic pattern into sound.

Magnetic field

A magnet's pull, or force, works in the area all around it. This area is called a magnetic field. Every magnet has two places where the force is strongest.

You can find these strong places by putting a magnet into a pile of small straight pins. Lift the magnet out carefully and see where most of the pins are sticking.

You cannot see a magnetic field. But you can find out where it is by using tiny pieces of iron called iron filings.

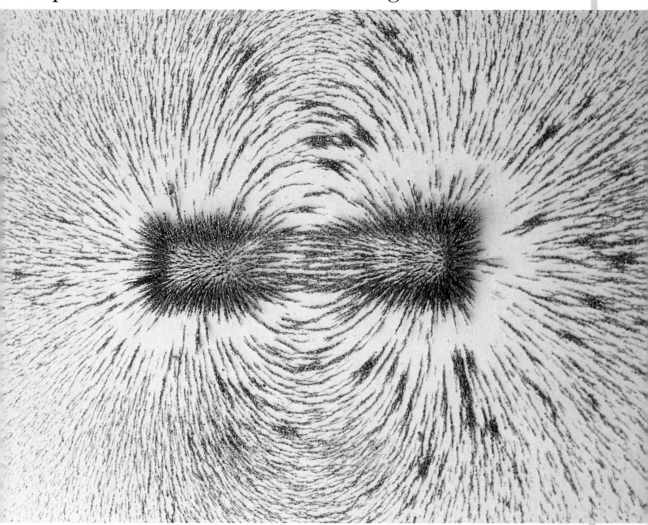

In this picture, filings have been sprinkled over a sheet of paper on top of a bar magnet. The filings clump together where the magnetic field is strongest.

Compasses

The Earth acts as if it has a magnet through its center. It has a magnetic field like other magnets, and north and south poles.

These students are using a compass to find out which direction they are going in.

The needle inside the compass is a magnet. One end always points to the Earth's magnetic north pole.

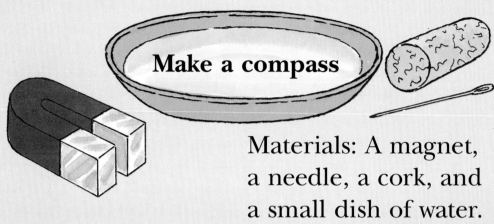

Make a compass

Materials: A magnet, a needle, a cork, and a small dish of water.

Hold the needle steady. Rub it with the magnet from one end to the other, always in the same direction.

Lift the magnet away from the needle between each rubbing.

Ask an adult to cut a groove in the cork. Lay the needle in the groove.

Float the cork in the water. How do you check that your needle points north and south?

North and south

The pull of a magnet is strongest at two points called north and south poles. A bar magnet has a pole at each end. A north pole and a south pole attract each other.

Two south poles push each other apart, or repel each other.

What do you think happens when two north poles are near each other?

Finding north and south

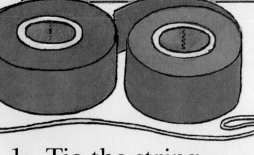

Materials: A bar magnet, string, blue and red masking tape and a compass.

1. Tie the string around the middle of the magnet.

2. Hang the magnet from a hook.

3. Put blue tape on the end that points south.

4. Put red tape on the end that points north.

Electromagnets

When electricity flows through a wire it makes a magnetic field around the wire. If you wrap the wire around an iron nail, the nail becomes a strong magnet. This kind of magnet, called an electromagnet, can be turned on and off.

If this boy takes a wire off the battery, the electricity will stop flowing and the paper clips will fall.

This crane has a powerful electromagnet attached to it. When the electricity is turned on, the electromagnet can pick up the heavy scrap iron. When it is turned off, the iron falls.

In the home

Electromagnets are used in many ways in the home. A telephone has an electromagnet inside.

When someone speaks to you on the phone, electricity flows through the electromagnet inside the phone. This moves a thin piece of metal up and down.

The movement makes the sounds that we hear.

An electric doorbell has an electromagnet. When you press the button, electricity flows through the electromagnet inside. This makes a hammer hit against a metal chime.

Motors and magnets

Electric motors have magnets inside them. This toy car has an electric motor that is powered by a battery.

Many machines in your home work with electric motors. The motor in a vacuum cleaner has electromagnets inside that spin around when the electricity is turned on.

Electric drills and food processors also have electric motors.

Think about... magnets

The first magnets were hard rocks called lodestone. Before compasses were invented, lodestones were used to find the way.

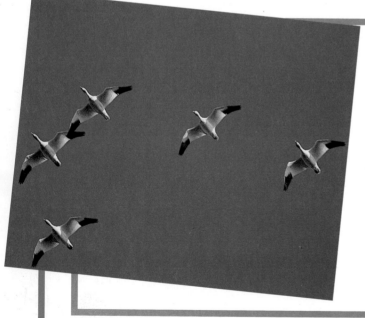

Scientists think that the Earth's magnetic field helps birds to find their way over long distances.

The maglev train has no wheels. It floats above the track. Magnets in the train and in the track repel each other.

Put a ball bearing onto a magnet. Add more ball bearings one at a time.

Hold the top ball bearing and lift the magnet slightly. The bearings still hang in a chain!

What happens if you move the magnet away?

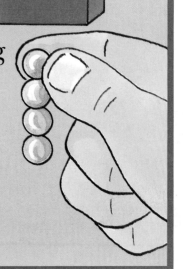

INDEX